Obliterations

OBLITERATIONS

Jessica Piazza &
Heather Aimee O'Neill

Red Hen Press | *Pasadena, CA*

Obliterations

Book layout by Hannah Nelson

Library of Congress Cataloging-in-Publication Data

Names: Piazza, Jessica, 1977– author. | O'Neill, Heather Aimee, 1976– author.
Title: Obliterations / Jessica Piazza & Heather Aimee O'Neill.
Description: Pasadena, CA : Red Hen Press, [2016]
Identifiers: LCCN 2015050370 | ISBN 9781597097406 (paperback)
Subjects: | BISAC: POETRY / General.
Classification: LCC PS3616.I213 A6 2016 | DDC 811/.6—dc23
LC record available at http://lccn.loc.gov/2015050370

The National Endowment for the Arts, the Los Angeles County Arts Commission, the Los Angeles Department of Cultural Affairs, the Dwight Stuart Youth Fund, the Pasadena Arts & Culture Commission and the City of Pasadena Cultural Affairs Division, Sony Pictures Entertainment, and the Ahmanson Foundation partially support Red Hen Press.

First Edition
Published by Red Hen Press
www.redhen.org

Acknowledgments

Thank you to the following journals and websites who first published these poems or versions of them:

Gingko Tree Review: "Crossing" and "Of Fire;" *Pith*: "Boundaries Without;" *THEthe Poetry (The Infoxicated Corner)*: "Slow Return," "Succumb To," "Temptation," and "That Crumpled;" *Ryga*: "Bomb," "Not About Anything," "Stalled Out," and "Woman Shattered;" *Southern Pacific Review*: "Compressed;" *TAB*: "Edit Yourself," "The End of And," "Regulate," and "You Might;" *Whale Road Review*: "Mud Stunning" and "Two Moons;" *Ginko Tree Review*.

We would also like to offer some personal thanks to certain individuals and organizations:

Heather Aimee O'Neill: Thank you to Jessica Piazza, who insisted we share a cup of coffee nearly twenty years ago after meeting in Eric McHenry's poetry class at Boston University. I am so grateful to the beautiful friendship and artistic collaborations that have emerged from that invitation. Thank you to the Lambda Literary Writers' Retreat for giving me both time and space to work on these poems. To the incredible team at Red Hen Press for believing in the project. To my family; I am so blessed to have you. To Caroline; my love, my yes, always. And to Tommy and Teo, you are beautiful boys and so very loved.

Jessica Piazza: I'd like to give Heather Aimee O'Neill all the thanks all the time, but since that's crazy I hope this will suffice: Heath, I'm so grateful for you and I adore our writing partnership almost as much as our amazing friendship. To my three families (Piazza, Jaroszewicz and Krane): I'm so thankful and so very lucky for you. To the family of friends that has grown through the years (you know who you are), you make it possible and you make it fun. So much thanks to Red Hen Press (especially Kate Gale and Mark E. Cull) for being supportive publishers as my career has grown. To all who have supported the Poetry Has Value project, thanks for your help. And to Artur, who gets it: I love you more than anything: XOP.

For our families . . .

Contents

Education

Books

Environment

Travel

Obituary

NY Region

Home and Garden: Domestic Lives

Movies

Fashion

Sports

Opinionator

Technology

Opinion Pages

Weddings and Celebrations

Automobile

Science

A note on the text:

The poems in *Obliterations* are all erasures, using articles from *The New York Times* as source texts.

The book is written by two authors; we took the same articles and wrote our own erasures of them without seeing the other's versions. In that sense, this project was not collaborative (excepting our collaborations with the articles themselves). Our main interest was highlighting the surprising similarities and differences that arise in works that share the same source material.

We kept the words from the articles in their original tenses, conjugations, and forms; we erased many words but none were added. The order of the words remains intact, though we added and removed punctuation and formatting at will.

We noted which part of the newspaper the source article came from in the table of contents and in the section headings at the top of each new set of poems. The article URLs, dates, titles, and authors are cited in the Notes section.

"The true picture of the past flits by. The past can be seized only as an image which flashes up at the instant when it can be recognized and is never seen again."

—Walter Benjamin
On the Concept of History

"The past is a great place and I don't want to erase it or to regret it, but I don't want to be its prisoner either."

—Mick Jagger
El País, November 4, 2001

Real Estate

That Crumpled

It was a tryst. It was a trip.
Difficult fiction. Certain collapse.

I do this all the time.

Collapsed. Back together.
No stable structure.

I collapsed. I collapse.
No one was hurt.

But I had to collapse.

Slow Return

It was a tryst with a woman,
supposedly.

It was a rush,
maybe.

It had tunnels that led
from inside out into,
probably.

This is clad in lore and embellishment,
but the facade tumbled along that long,
long road—two kids, partner, furniture,
mementos in storage. I collapsed.
They did, too.

The façade.
This façade.

I had to be rebuilt from the ground up,
and while portions could be saved
almost everything else had to be
reconstructed.

Closed for so many years,
sleepy,
vanishing,
nobody.

Now, bare, I move.
I know what's happening
downstairs.

There are windows!

A door.
            Life.

People want that.

Magazine

Sorry

I'd trade in this evening,
splintered and arched skyward,

but I need brutal language
to feel alive. I'd follow this moment

of apotheosis, but I don't
need you. I'm right.

I need you. I'm wrong.
I know you

understand the battlefield:
love. But also my flaws,

my venom. I have been
a long way from home.

I've had to battle the things
that make you

you. I believe
I have you, still.

Not About Anything

Light the color of stone. A box.
A mocking plaza. Burlap sacks
over black robes, ecstatically rolled eyes.

In this heroic melody, a devilish whistle.
Life is cheap. Life is cheap.

If this is what he needs to feel
alive—a carpet-bomb, punches,
a scathing end—he is among friends.

He is wooing the valuable battlefield.
Those who stand and those who love
destructive pleasure.

The greatest scandal in history
is small talk. A big, public life
fraught with golden flaws. A city's
exhausting fear. A state insane.

There is no being kind.
Life is cheap.

Health

Living with Dark

Before, I slept.

Now, I wake
in the dark, my body
misused, love squandered.
I hold my fear so fiercely
in the ghastly night.

Speak to me about blessings or
silence my stories, my failures.

I don't want to be one.
I don't want to need.

I need to go back to love.

I am awakening
to my fate. There is life
to abide with, not blight.

The streak of light at night
reminds me
to see.

Living Dark

A slant of light bifurcates the night, light silvering
the night, shaft of light and time, stalled sight.

Waking in the dark, dark night I wake
tense as a verb. Ghastly night, a heightened

bitterness. Hard not to feel, or fail.
Harder still, my scarred attachments.

I don't want this witching hour. I need
a line to love, to slow sleep. Not to wake

again too soon. A trick, a tune awakening
my sleep. Slow. Slow. I learn by going.

Waking to the streak of light. At night
the eye begins to see.

Space and Cosmos

Woman Shattered

To fly was the cause, was the mission, was the explosion and crash. She said: *I'm cut*. She said: *broken*. She had already made a commitment, but still.

She politely focused on her plan to cry.

She would be bad.
Too bad.

In her early days, trained in weightlessness, she learned to fly. She chose space. She watched little girls in flight and learned to be revealing, shunned the reserved and reticent. The only disaster was that people had forgotten. Learned disintegration, insulation.

But she flew, twice. Twice, she lost.

The year floated away. She kept her secret. She fought for logic, and was devastated. When she wanted, she was homesick. When she laughed, her secret survived.

What drove her was not desire. All she wanted to do was fly.

Shattered Space

At home, I'm in movement,
paved by a commitment
to flight. A barrage of questions

on reproductive organs,
children, makeup, menstruation,
and shoes.

Two women. One came.
A cosmonaut trained in weightlessness.
The shuttle landed.

Suspended by the—O—
          a cold morning,
          a troubled time,
          a gashed wing.

I flew to a lunar outpost.
The stars showed there are limits
to home. It's no secret I desire

to become, to soar,
float inside the place
she was meant to be.

Education

Healing

So haunted, we don't forget
the exact color of that red.

Toward Healing

Glass glistens. Walls flower.
These spaces were once other things.

Not yet haunted, they were
unrecognizable. The painful processes,

though, happened. A growing crime
remade to resemble the old violence.

A need moving toward tragedy. A child.
A returning to the same terror.

Get over it. Anything you want
to get rid of: demolish.

A room could become a shrine.
Unwanted quiet, a new hope.

A found scene converted into
a whole new anthropology

of the spirit.

Books

With Two

You follow her
lead, the quicksand

of mouth, the passages
startlingly irresistible,

mysterious. A chrysalis
will surely create

a chrysalis. And so,
the incantatory longing

goes on.

Two Moons

Don't make close comparisons.
Those two moons have a fixation.

They echo one another, incantatory.
We learn and we learn. We learn

and we learn that the second moon
is mostly a centerpiece—large and fearsome—

but has powers that keep the world afloat.
Some cosmic balance in this magnitude.

Environment

Sex

We've found the purpose of creation:

new combinations
plants   animals   microbes
wine   industry   disease

resistance.

Vulnerable as
a seedling:

the desired,

the desired! We follow

the taste beyond to thrive
fully,
ripen,
make.

Sex Tangles

For the last 8,000 years:
very little sex. Abstinence

threatens to sap the pleasure
of millions. The reason,

obvious: breaking off
a shoot and sticking it in

is favored. Sexual reproduction
has not been novel.

~

The new method: flowering,
looking, leading.

Shifting to new
taste. Ample wine.

Many surprises. Pursuit.
His wife to thrive,

fully ripen. The fantastic,
sparkling good.

Travel

Mud Stunning

My first coastline, composed
of fearsome weather.

We were available
and reassured.

We decided to squander
and shuttle. Idyllic hours.

We strolled among dunes,
above the crashing.

We woke to gentle comfort,
then set out along the beach.

The possible stretches,
long and dense.

Since those days, the shifting
tides. We reached the waves

and the waves intensified.
The weather worsened,

the worst yet to come.
We faced an endless

existential why. An inevitable
struggle, a destination

we took off to. Up and down,
string and safety, we tried.

We found a path, a puzzle deep
and wide and trickier than we expected.

The world turned half better,
as we marveled at the rain.

Mud and Beauty

Shipwrecked sailors,
we decided: here we end.

That first day was idyllic.
A sheltered grove, trees, the sun
set, a beach, crashing waves.

The next morning, a surprise:
rains, coastal cliffs, impassable
forest, mountain ranges,
dense scrub.

Still, the discovery.
Why were we here?

We approached the end.
We cursed. We marveled.
We stopped to look back,

then realized what it meant
                    to fall.

Obituary

Bomb

The nuclear tonight
advanced.

Since the first shadow
of the world's first sunlike
flash:

—The age of fabrication
and misgivings.

Brilliant tongues, exploded
implications, unleashing

clouds of splendor and death.
Some sort of sin. A knowledge
they cannot lose.

—The age of the father,
of praise and eminence.

A blank wall stripped
of charm, violently authentic,
echoing knowledge.

—The age of decline and fall,
of massive experiences, compulsive culture.

Art was delicate work. Sciences,
a celebrated ivory-tower, almost
wholly divorced from its gravity.

A change of direction that added
sinister overtones to the awakening
world.

A love affair, now dead.

A continuing fury that unified
the immense, tension-filled world.

Atom Bomb Pioneer

The flash told a story
in tongues that exploded
the universe, flashed
as if the suns burst
into black.

I have known sin,
he offered.

NY Region

Snowfall Blankets

The seaboard swirled with still-
fresh memories of that paralyzed city,

streets unplowed. This time around,
salt spreaders, wide plows on the ground.

Midmorning, the giant amoeba-
shaped storm touched down.

Central Park braced for punishment,
bright cityscape, window sills framed by white,

water towers like brand-new caps.
Snow fell.

Snowfall Flights

A storm tore across, forcing:
storm-shaped snowstorm

pummeling hundreds.
Scrubbed buses.

Volcanoes of weather mess
inching along dozens of districts.

A disrupted

city
laggardly left

standing by. Fending off.
Salted.

Help.   Help now.
The city tunnels out of the night.

Not an emergency.
A declaration.

Home and Garden: Domestic Lives

Vanish

Our dismay encouraged us to turn
to God. We found ourselves
less in the way. Where I come

from, delving into something
so intimate is hunger,
religion, envy. But after

we'd all but given up
hope, we allowed
ourselves the resurrection,
the only one: home.

Chicken Ensues

Chickens live sheltered lives.
Chickens are public figures.
Chickens decamping in New York
to feed on the energy of admirers.
In droves. Immortalized. Conscious
and nostalgic. There's an awful lot
of love, happy hiccup of feathers,
the ceaseless melancholy of
the weary spirit, gently corrected.

Chickens make people loose.
Chickens are important.

Chickens aren't usually important.
Imagine the chicken yard, open to friends,
to public pleading. As with any faith.

Chickens of goodwill, of God.
Neighbors comforted. The odds, good.

Chicken,

if I digress—confused about the great pleasures
of living, the abstract or esoteric musings
intimate hunger promised to all—dare to return.

Return to marvel
at the Snake
among the good citizens.

Movies

The Past Is

You risk
risk—or show

that she echoes
across time and space,

that there are ruptures
where once there was a path,

that death suggests
something simpler,

that nature is you and me
and you and you.

It's everything,
but what we wanted to be.

The Present Is Uninvited

She helped him navigate a breakthrough
under his bed. Never conventional.

But now a final risk, artistic risk, a way to show
generations a shared history: *kinship, end.*

The wife defied convention.
Sex, a jealous keeper, tortured by time,
female and censored.

It's different now.
There's an uneasy partnership
And you see the ruptures.

The work of independence remains
a fraught subject, a problem, hot
conflicts. Startling one,
the other destroyed.

They lose the symbol
to safeguard the image.

He said: I don't want to be someone
bigger than this.

He has his devious strategies.

He said: Kill, kill.
The whole thing is very poetic.

They were looking to achieve something timeless.
Synthesis of everything.

But not that.

Fashion

In an Era without Any

I did not mind
not knowing.
The retouches we live
in are like a curiosity
that has lost its allure.

We still have sex. It's become
natural once more—not just
manipulation to get you
to wonder, to widen.

Boundaries Without

A parallel wife,
a friend, a wife,
two girls: a story
of fashion.

A parallel universe
rather than real.

Each of us has nothing
significant to say.

We live dull taboos,
zippered bodies.

Approach and known. A skeleton
with sadomasochistic years.

It is hard to look without seeing.
To explore the hot extreme.

A guiding focus
on the narrow:
livelier, more daring
than power.

People turn
their bodies, still.

Carbon portraits
of pretty.

A pill
and blue skin.

Sports

Crossing

I decided it would be fun.
It was morning, and my connection

to a new world opened. Wonder
in the lengths I would go: a heavy,

hard kind of travel, the sort of going
that might risk raucous, buzzing tension.

I didn't quit. Trudging, moving slowly.
Didn't quit, relentless locomotion.

That was every day. I took my time with him.
Such a thrill, what we do for us.

To See

Home. I wanted nothing more
than to leave.

I faded right down hills,
up hills,
            cambered turns.

Lost a shoe.

But, Lord,
I didn't quit.

I have often
wondered why.

Dining

Temptation

I'm here, ever-
present.

Pulling hard,
I resisted,

but gave in.

The first change
was to use the word:

You.

Succumb To

I'm here
to persuade you.

The urge, pulling
hard.

I resisted, but
couldn't.

I gave in
to the filling

up, the fallen under,
the spiked craving.

The half-tender,
perfect: *if.*

You could.
You don't want to.

You could.
You want to.

Politics

Female, Still

A one-woman tornado hunting
a small indulgence, consumed

by kids, insurance, school, taxes,
the price of something
God intended to happen.
                                        Mythmaking.

Now settled. The remaining
part of her works a second job.

She seeks one slice
of the much sliced and diced day.

Crucial Female

Hunting a torn promise,
spinning and seized.

Winning but vanished
women.

Moveable opposition.

A battleground
like this needs:

volatile women
interesting women

important women
kaleidoscopic

as any fascinating men.

Music

Earth, Compressed By

Society was dedicated,
earnest. The vanity
of earth, infused
with life and white light,
a cohesive whole.

Earthly life: a long,
dirge-like interlude.
Alongside foaming climaxes,
dabs of exotic color.

~

Stripped of underlying architecture,
emotions are magnified. Desolate
moments, bleak and hopeful. Poignant,
compared to a painting, a woodcut.

But so jagged, the lurid
howling of garish bright light.
Explosive, dangerous,
rattling alienation.

~

The relationships felt in
autumn loneliness
become like strangers
warily circling one another.

Here is earth
and song of the earth.
Pried apart, heightened
and sharpened.

In the expressive power
of the trembling of the earth,
the existential shiver
of man.

Compressed

Celebrate the pleasures
                    of movement,

passages
                    howling within the dissonances.

The loneliness of love rises
in the farewell,

meandering lines separate,

strangers circling one another,
pried apart

under a microscope.

In doing so,
a new harmony.

Home and Garden: The Pragmatist

Preventing Heat

Your house breathes.
My house doesn't breathe.

I'll explain: air is escaping.
My home has enough caulk

to seal a ship. A leak is easy.

In your home, I missed spots.
I hadn't thought to check

the seam between your access.
I never considered the effect,

that sag. All your piping is coming
and going. Things happen:

your house might settle and open.
You may detect cracks,

the day shining through.
Every place I've ever lived

has had a front door.
Your threshold breaks down

less easily than foam.
I learned how my home

exhales, all the leaks
I missed.

Sneaking

Fact breathes.

A typical exhale, every hour, breathe.
Hyperventilate.

Every hour: purge, kill, set free.
I explain where   the air is

escaping,
holes and leaks,
stripping my
every hour.

Tricks:

a breezy day
and any seam

is the biggest omission.

US

Ocean of Firearms

The question why spilled out of the day
and traipsed through fields of memory,

the expanse of we. Oh, they looked.
They had been instructed to

have no opinion about the carnage.
That's like pointing a finger

at a hurricane. (Everyone wants to
get shutters; it doesn't make a difference.)

The fears about where we are remain
ever in the things we've seen.

People didn't seem surprised.

Of Fire

In a sea of thousands, there was something
to the sprawling, rejected people.

Parents, friends, teachers, the decline,
the failure or absence.

A breakdown of convention, of
the camouflage of doubt I control.

I have no control. I thank vigorously,
point at the passers-by, examine

the reaction after injuries. I make much
of good and remain ever vigilant in case

the scary things we've read, the things
we've seen, over-take the details.

Opinionator

Undead

The imminent demise
approaches predictably.

Pick your reasons:
I'm not sure / I'm certain.

This is typical.

In my early life, I did my part
to keep living.

A raging kept me.
I built a strong body,
intuited, never questioned.

My, how things have changed.

We need and provide.
We manage neither.

The Undead

The Hostess met millions who thought a lot.
The Hostess never pretended to like them.

And you can hardly blame a Hostess for negotiating
with memory, surreptitiously filling in a soft surrounding,
a close dark diversion, unadulterated . . .

—unless you count how the Hostess manufactured it.
Intuited that adult eyes never questioned sweets.

The Hostess ruled the world.
The Hostess produces the demise.
The tune sung. The crisis resolved.

Technology

Years of Edit

Across the beautiful affection
remains much work to be done.

Native language of all,
we're missing the drive to open.

The lesson we are to become.

Edit Yourself

Regular people live with no fanfare, suffer
inaccuracies and hoaxes, celebrate with parties
and beautiful, awkward affection.

Amateurs.

The sum total of all human knowledge
—in India, in Egypt and Brazil, universities
and museums, breaking news—

was a warning.

Opinion Pages

Why

We are awash in civil war,
barely a whisker of hope.

Boom.

Bloodbath.

You shot.

I reload.

Regulate

He rejected cars and toys,
medicines and mutual funds.

Boy with a gun,

awash in minor
hopes of being safer.

The evidence
is overwhelming.

A forecast clear as the cracked
wrist halved. Echoed but hollow

memorial.

Weddings and Celebrations

It's the Feel

Who wanted myth?

It boils down to something
romantic: a beginning.

Just another couple
        who love. I can't

help but be drawn
to the end.

The End of And

Some choose to marry, date,
be still. Others are wed

to doomsday. Some were in China,
Minneapolis, Belize, thumbing their noses
at the world.

Wanted a destination.
Wanted myth, something
banal, easy.

For those who were convinced:
Hollywood.

Those who saw an end
were drawn to fashion
and spiritual symbolism;

thought: *a perfect day, a new life,*
a tiny just-in-case.

All said: *I wouldn't want to share.*

Automobile

Stalled Out

A fast-charging, ultrafast
charging reality seemed

ideal. Charging by, a fast-
charge to a luminous day;

a charge with energy
and stretch.

I meant: dispensing
with anxiety.

That advice
was wrong.

My knuckles were white
from the effort.

On

I discovered the plunge
along the coast, a new range

for silent wonder. I crossed
that stretch, battery-draining,

the woman who told me to
turn, told me—
                    now!

I advanced well beyond
the distance I intended

to cover.
Rescue me.

Science

You Already Know

On a crusade,
you discover reason.
What are the odds

that does not exist?

You Might . . .

. . . have seen it coming in recent weeks,
taking heat from many minds, many hearts
inflamed with biases, saving themselves.

Embarrassment brought this whole subject up
again. I could devote my entire life to it:

testing the risk, measuring the effect,
the color of a word, the word and color.
And everyone you are measuring

is small. Anything you discover is slightly
weighted toward *yes*. A fair coin, any probability
the probability of rough odds, weighed against

what is observable in the world.

Notes

The URLs for The New York Times articles we used are listed below, along with their titles, authors and dates, in the order they appear in the book.

"Slow Return for a Former Speakeasy That Crumpled" by Elizabeth A. Harris, REAL ESTATE, December 31, 2012. http://www.nytimes.com/2013/01/01/nyregion/chumleys-ex-speakeasy-in-greenwich-village-seems-on-mend.html?ref=realestate

"Martin Peretz Is Not Sorry. About Anything." by Stephen Rodrick, MAGAZINE, January 24, 2011. http://www.nytimes.com/2011/01/30/magazine/30Peretz-t.html

"Living With Cancer: Waking in the Dark" by Susan Gubar, HEALTH, February 07, 2013. http://well.blogs.nytimes.com/2013/02/07/living-with-cancer-waking-in-the-dark/?ref=health

"American Woman Who Shattered Space Ceiling" by Denise Grady, SPACE & COSMOS, July 23, 2012. http://www.nytimes.com/2012/07/24/science/space/sally-ride-trailblazing-astronaut-dies-at-61.html

"Varied Paths Toward Healing for Sites of Terrorized Schools" by Winnie Hu, EDUCATION, December 21, 2012. http://www.nytimes.com/2012/12/22/nyregion/after-rampages-officials-often-give-schools-different-life.html?ref=education

"A Tokyo With Two Moons and Many More Puzzles" by Janet Maslin, BOOKS, November 9, 2011. http://www.nytimes.com/2011/11/10/books/1q84-by-haruki-murakami-review.html

"Lack of Sex Among Grapes Tangles a Family Vine" by Nicholas Wade, ENVIRONMENT, January 24, 2011. http://www.nytimes.com/2011/01/25/science/25wine.html

"Mud, Leeches and Stunning Beauty in Tasmania" by Alex Hutchinson, TRAVEL, January 25, 2013. http://travel.nytimes.com/2013/01/27/travel/mud-leeches-and-stunning-beauty-in-tasmania.html?ref=travel

"J. Robert Oppenheimer, Atom Bomb Pioneer, Dies" by Staff, OBITUARY, February 19, 1967. http://www.nytimes.com/learning/general/onthisday/bday/0422.html

"Snowfall Blankets Region and Snarls Flights" by James Barron and Anahad O'Connor, NEW YORK REGION, January 11, 2011. http://www.nytimes.com/2011/01/12/nyregion/12snow.html

"Chicken Vanishes, Heartbreak Ensues" by Elizabeth Giddens, HOME & GARDEN, February 2, 2011. http://www.nytimes.com/2011/02/03/garden/03domestic.html?src=me&ref=homepage

"The Past Is Always Present, Even Uninvited (Films From the Arab World at MoMA)" by John Anderson, MOVIES, October 26, 2012. http://www.nytimes.com/2012/10/28/movies/films-from-the-arab-world-at-moma.html?ref=arts&_r=0

"Pushing Fashion Boundaries in an Era Without Any" by Cathy Horyn, FASHION, January 13, 2011. http://www.nytimes.com/2011/01/13/fashion/13NOTEBOOK.html

"Crossing the Ocean to See a One-of-a-Kind Horse" by Paul Rutherford, SPORTS, October 27, 2012. http://www.nytimes.com/2012/10/28/sports/crossing-the-atlantic-to-see-the-superhorse-frankel.html

"You Can Succumb to a Sticky Temptation" by Melissa Clark, DINING, January 4, 2013. http://www.nytimes.com/2013/01/09/dining/glazed-cinnamon-rolls-are-a-sticky-temptation.html?ref=dining

"Crucial Subset: Female Voters Still Deciding" by Katharine Q. Seelye, POLITICS, October 24, 2012. http://www.nytimes.com/2012/10/25/us/politics/female-swing-voters-a-coveted-demographic.html

"Mahler's 'Earth,' Compressed By Schoenberg" by Corinna Da Fonesca Wollheim, MUSIC, October 26, 2012. http://www.nytimes.com/2012/10/28/arts/music/schoenbergs-version-of-mahlers-song-of-the-earth.html?ref=arts

"Preventing Heat From Sneaking Out of the House" by Bob Tedeschi, HOME & GARDEN, January 12, 2011. http://www.nytimes.com/2011/01/13/garden/13prag.html

"In an Ocean of Firearms, Tucson Is Far Away" by Adam Nagourney, US, January 19, 2011. http://www.nytimes.com/2011/01/20/us/20guns.html

Twinkies, the Undead Snack by Mark Bittman, THE OPINIONATOR, January 17, 2012.
http://opinionator.blogs.nytimes.com/2012/01/17/twinkies-the-undead-snack/

"Wikipedia Marks 10 Years of Edit-It-Yourself" by Verne G. Kopytoff, TECHNOLOGY, January 13, 2011. http://bits.blogs.nytimes.com/2011/01/13/wikipedia-marks-10-years-of-edit-it-yourself/

"Why Not Regulate Guns as Seriously as Toys?" by Nicholas D. Kristof, THE OPINION PAGES, January 12, 2011. http://www.nytimes.com/2011/01/13/opinion/13kristof.html

"It's the End of the World and I Feel Fine" by Margaux Laskey, WEDDINGS AND CELEBRATIONS, December 21, 2012. http://www.nytimes.com/2012/12/23/fashion/weddings/amid-talk-of-the-mayan-calendar-ending-getting-married-is-a-beginning-for-many-couples.html?ref=weddings

"Stalled Out on Tesla's Electric Highway" by John M. Broder, AUTOMOBILES, February 8, 2013. http://www.nytimes.com/2013/02/10/automobiles/stalled-on-the-ev-highway.html?ref=automobiles&_r=0

"You Might Already Know This . . ." by Benedict Carey, SCIENCE, January 10, 2011. http://www.nytimes.com/2011/01/11/science/11esp.html

Biographical Note

JESSICA PIAZZA is the author of two previous poetry collections, including *Interrobang* (Red Hen Press, 2013), which won AROHO's To The Lighthouse Poetry Publication Prize.

HEATHER AIMEE O'NEILL teaches creative writing at CUNY Hunter College and the Sackett Street Writers' Workshop. Her previous poetry collection, *Memory Future*, won the University of Southern California's Gold Line Press Award, chosen by judge Carol Muske-Dukes, Poet Laureate of California.